BHARAT

REDEFINED GEOPOLITICALLY

PRANJAL GUHA

DEDICATION

This book is dedicated to the vibrant spirit, rich culture, and indomitable resilience of our nation. Bharat, with its diversity of languages, cultures, and traditions, has always been a source of inspiration and pride for its people.

In writing this book, I am deeply grateful for the countless individuals who have contributed to shaping Bharat's identity and destiny. From the freedom fighters who sacrificed their lives for our independence to the visionaries who have worked tirelessly to build a better future, Bharat's journey is a testament to the power of determination, unity, and perseverance.

To the brave men and women of our armed forces who safeguard our sovereignty and protect our borders, this book is dedicated to your unwavering courage and sacrifice. Your selfless service and dedication inspire us all to strive for excellence and uphold the values of peace, freedom, and democracy.

To the farmers who toil in the fields to feed our nation, this book is dedicated to your hard work, resilience, and dedication. Your labor sustains us all and reminds us of the importance of respecting and nurturing the land that sustains us.

DP PUBLICATION INDIA

To the teachers who ignite the flames of curiosity and knowledge in young minds, this book is dedicated to your passion, dedication, and commitment to shaping the future leaders of our nation. Your guidance and mentorship empower us to reach new heights and realize our full potential.

To the entrepreneurs and innovators who drive Bharat's economic growth and prosperity, this book is dedicated to your creativity, ingenuity, and vision. Your innovative spirit and entrepreneurial drive propel Bharat forward and inspire us all to embrace change and seize opportunities.

To the women of Bharat who embody strength, grace, and resilience, this book is dedicated to your courage, determination, and leadership. Your contributions to every aspect of our society are invaluable, and your voices deserve to be heard and celebrated.

To the youth of Bharat who hold the key to our nation's future, this book is dedicated to your passion, energy, and idealism. Your creativity, innovation, and commitment to social justice and equality inspire hope and promise for a brighter tomorrow.

Finally, to Bharat itself, the land of my birth and the cradle of civilization, this book is dedicated to your timeless beauty, boundless diversity, and eternal spirit. May we always cherish and protect the legacy of our ancestors and work together to build a Bharat that is inclusive, prosperous, and at peace with itself and the world.

With love, gratitude, and pride,

Pranjal Guha

PREFACE

Bharat: Redefined Geopolitically

In a world of shifting alliances, emerging powers, and geopolitical complexities, Bharat stands at a crossroads, poised to redefine its role and influence on the global stage. "Bharat: Redefined Geopolitically" is a groundbreaking book that explores the dynamic interplay of politics, economics, culture, and geography that shapes Bharat's position in the world.

At its core, this book seeks to unravel the complexities of Bharat's geopolitical landscape and shed light on the opportunities and challenges that lie ahead. Drawing on a wealth of research, analysis, and firsthand insights, "Bharat: Redefined Geopolitically" offers a comprehensive examination of Bharat's strategic imperatives, regional dynamics, and global aspirations.

The book begins by delving into the historical foundations of Bharat's geopolitical identity, tracing its evolution from ancient civilizations to modern nationhood. It explores the enduring legacies of Bharat's cultural heritage, spiritual traditions, and philosophical insights that continue to shape its worldview and interactions with the world.

From there, the book examines Bharat's strategic imperatives in the 21st century, considering factors such as security challenges, economic opportunities, and diplomatic engagements. It analyzes Bharat's strategic partnerships with key regional and global players, exploring how these alliances shape Bharat's geopolitical calculus and influence its decision-making processes.

One of the key themes explored in the book is Bharat's emergence as a leading global power in the 21st century. It examines Bharat's economic rise, technological prowess, and diplomatic engagements, highlighting how these factors contribute to Bharat's growing influence and stature on the world stage.

However, the book also delves into the challenges and complexities that Bharat faces in navigating the global geopolitical landscape. From border disputes and regional rivalries to economic disparities and social tensions, Bharat grapples with a myriad of issues that impact its security, stability, and prosperity.

Moreover, "Bharat: Redefined Geopolitically" goes beyond mere analysis to offer bold insights and policy prescriptions for Bharat's future trajectory. It explores innovative approaches to diplomacy, economic development, and regional cooperation that can help Bharat realize its full potential and become a leading force for peace, stability, and prosperity in the region and beyond.

One of the unique features of the book is its emphasis on Bharat's soft power and cultural diplomacy as tools for enhancing its geopolitical influence. It explores Bharat's rich cultural heritage, vibrant democracy, and diverse society as sources of strength and resilience that can help Bharat forge deeper connections with other nations and peoples.

Throughout the book, the voices of Bharat's youth are prominently featured, providing fresh perspectives and innovative ideas for navigating the challenges of the 21st century. From digital innovation and sustainable development to social justice and human rights, Bharat's youth are at the forefront of shaping the nation's future and redefining its role in the world.

In conclusion, "Bharat: Redefined Geopolitically" is a seminal work that offers a comprehensive and insightful exploration of Bharat's evolving geopolitical landscape. With its blend of rigorous analysis, bold insights, and visionary thinking, this book is essential reading for anyone seeking to understand Bharat's place in the world and the forces shaping its future.

Source:

- Ministry of External Affairs, Government of Bharat: https://www.mea.gov.in/
- Institute for Defence Studies and Analyses (IDSA): https://idsa.in/
- Centre for Policy Research (CPR): https://www.cprindia.org/
- Brookings Institution India: https://www.brookings.edu/india/
- Observer Research Foundation (ORF): https://www.orfonline.org/
- Carnegie India: https://carnegieindia.org/
- The Hindu: https://www.thehindu.com/
- Hindustan Times: https://www.hindustantimes.com/
- Economic and Political Weekly (EPW): https://www.epw.in/
- Centre for Strategic and International Studies (CSIS): https://www.csis.org/
- Council on Foreign Relations (CFR): https://www.cfr.org/
- Royal United Services Institute (RUSI): https://rusi.org/
- International Institute for Strategic Studies (IISS): https://www.iiss.org/

INDEX

1

INTRODUCTION

Geopolitics is the study of how geographical factors, political dynamics, and economic considerations intersect to shape the power dynamics between nations. It encompasses an understanding of how resources, borders, and strategic locations influence a country's foreign policy decisions and its position in the global arena.

Geopolitics plays a crucial role in determining a nation's standing in the world. Factors such as military strength, economic prowess, diplomatic alliances, and cultural influence all contribute to a country's geopolitical power. Nations strive to enhance their geopolitical influence through various means, including military expansion, economic partnerships, and soft power diplomacy.

The current global situation presents both opportunities and challenges for Bharat. On one hand, globalization has opened up new avenues for economic growth and international cooperation. Bharat's growing economy, young population, and strategic location position it favorably to capitalize on global trade and investment opportunities. Additionally, advancements in technology and communication have enabled Bharat to play an increasingly prominent role in the digital economy and global innovation ecosystem.

However, the current global landscape also poses significant challenges for Bharat. Geopolitical tensions in regions such as South Asia and the Indo-Pacific present security threats and diplomatic complexities for Bharat. Rising protectionism and trade disputes among major global powers could impact Bharat's export-oriented economy. Furthermore, environmental challenges such as climate change and resource scarcity require concerted international efforts to address, posing both environmental and economic risks for Bharat.

As a teenager, I see Bharat's role in the world as multifaceted and dynamic. My generation views Bharat as a nation with immense potential and aspirations for global leadership across various domains. We are proud of Bharat's rich cultural heritage, scientific achievements, and contributions to global peace and development.

However, we also recognize the challenges that Bharat faces in realizing its full potential on the world stage. Issues such as poverty, inequality, corruption, and environmental degradation continue to hinder Bharat's progress and impact its global standing. As teenagers, we are eager to contribute to addressing these challenges and shaping a more prosperous and sustainable future for Bharat.

We believe that Bharat has a unique role to play in promoting peace, prosperity, and cooperation on the global stage. Through diplomacy, innovation, and inclusive development strategies, Bharat can emerge as a leader in addressing pressing global issues such as climate change, poverty alleviation, and healthcare access.

In conclusion, geopolitics plays a critical role in shaping Bharat's standing in the world. The current global situation presents both opportunities and challenges for Bharat, requiring strategic foresight and proactive engagement to navigate. As teenagers, we are optimistic about Bharat's potential and eager to contribute to its progress and prosperity on the world stage. By leveraging our talents, creativity, and passion, we can work towards realizing Bharat's vision of becoming a leading global power that upholds principles of peace, inclusivity, and sustainable development.

2
ECONOMY

To provide a comprehensive analysis of Bharat's economic strengths, weaknesses, and its path to becoming a stronger economic power, we need to delve into various aspects of its economy, including its current status, challenges, and potential strategies for growth. Additionally, we'll explore the impact of globalization and trade on Bharat's economy, supported by relevant data and credible sources.

1. Introduction to Bharat's Economy:

Bharat, with its large and diverse economy, is one of the fastest-growing major economies in the world. Its strengths lie in its significant market size, a young and dynamic workforce, a growing middle class, and a vibrant entrepreneurial culture. However, Bharat also faces several challenges, including income inequality, infrastructure deficits, bureaucratic hurdles, and a high rate of informal employment.

2. Economic Strengths of Bharat:

a. Market Size: Bharat's large population of over 1.3 billion people makes it one of the largest consumer markets globally. This market size presents immense opportunities for businesses across various sectors, including consumer goods, retail, healthcare, and technology.

b. Young Workforce: Bharat has a youthful population, with a median age of around 28 years. This demographic dividend provides a significant advantage in terms of labor force participation, productivity, and innovation.

c. **Diverse Economy:** Bharat's economy is diverse, with strengths in agriculture, manufacturing, services, and information technology. This diversification helps mitigate risks and ensures resilience against external shocks.

d. **Entrepreneurial Culture:** Bharat has a vibrant entrepreneurial ecosystem, with a burgeoning startup ecosystem and a culture that encourages innovation and risk-taking. This fosters creativity, fosters job creation, and drives economic growth.

3. Economic Weaknesses of Bharat:

a. **Income Inequality:** Despite economic growth, Bharat grapples with significant income inequality, with a large portion of the population still living below the poverty line. This inequality poses social challenges and hampers inclusive growth.

b. **Infrastructure Deficits:** Bharat faces infrastructure deficits in areas such as transportation, energy, and urban development. Inadequate infrastructure hinders productivity, increases logistics costs, and limits the potential for economic expansion.

c. Bureaucratic Hurdles: Complex regulatory frameworks, bureaucratic red tape, and a slow decision-making process impede business growth and investment in Bharat. Streamlining administrative processes and improving governance are essential to foster a more business-friendly environment.

d. Informal Employment: A significant portion of Bharat's workforce is employed in the informal sector, lacking job security, social protection, and access to formal financial services. Formalizing the informal economy is crucial to improve labor productivity and promote inclusive growth.

4. Strategies for Strengthening Bharat's Economy:

a. Investment in Infrastructure: Bharat must prioritize investment in infrastructure development to address deficits and unlock growth potential. This includes enhancing transportation networks, expanding energy infrastructure, and improving urban amenities.

b. **Skill Development and Education:** Investing in education and skill development is essential to harness Bharat's demographic dividend. Enhancing access to quality education, vocational training, and lifelong learning opportunities can equip the workforce with the skills needed for the future economy.

c. **Ease of Doing Business Reforms:** Bharat should focus on simplifying regulatory processes, reducing bureaucratic hurdles, and improving the ease of doing business. Creating a conducive environment for entrepreneurship and investment will spur innovation, job creation, and economic growth.

d. **Promotion of Digital Economy:** Embracing digital technologies and promoting digital literacy can unlock new opportunities for Bharat's economy. Digital initiatives such as Digital Bharat, Make in Bharat, and Bharat Stack aim to digitize processes, improve efficiency, and foster innovation across sectors.

5. Impact of Globalization and Trade on Bharat's Economy:

a. Trade Liberalization: Bharat has witnessed significant trade liberalization reforms over the past few decades, leading to increased integration into the global economy. Trade agreements such as the Comprehensive Economic Partnership Agreement (CEPA) and Regional Comprehensive Economic Partnership (RCEP) aim to enhance trade relations and boost exports.

b. Foreign Direct Investment (FDI): Globalization has facilitated greater inflows of foreign direct investment (FDI) into Bharat, particularly in sectors such as information technology, manufacturing, and services. FDI inflows contribute to capital formation, technology transfer, and job creation in Bharat.

c. Global Value Chains: Bharat is increasingly participating in global value chains (GVCs), whereby goods and services are produced across different countries, creating efficiencies and specialization. Integration into GVCs offers opportunities for Bharat to enhance competitiveness, access new markets, and upgrade technology.

d. Challenges of Protectionism: However, Bharat also faces challenges posed by rising protectionism and trade tensions in the global arena. Trade disputes, tariffs, and non-tariff barriers hinder Bharat's export-oriented growth and disrupt supply chains.

6. Conclusion: In conclusion, Bharat possesses significant economic strengths, including its large market size, young workforce, diverse economy, and entrepreneurial culture. However, it also faces challenges such as income inequality, infrastructure deficits, bureaucratic hurdles, and informal employment. To become a stronger economic power, Bharat must prioritize investment in infrastructure, education, and skill development, streamline regulatory processes, and promote innovation and entrepreneurship.

Globalization and trade present both opportunities and challenges for Bharat's economy. While trade liberalization, FDI inflows, and participation in global value chains offer opportunities for growth and integration, rising protectionism and trade tensions pose risks to Bharat's export-oriented growth model. Addressing these challenges requires proactive policies, strategic reforms, and international cooperation to navigate the complexities of the global economy and ensure sustainable economic development for Bharat.

Sources:

World Bank: https://www.worldbank.org/en/country/india/overview

Reserve Bank of India: https://www.rbi.org.in/

Ministry of Commerce and Industry, Government of India: https://commerce.gov.in/

NITI Aayog: https://niti.gov.in/

International Monetary Fund (IMF): https://www.imf.org/en/Countries/IND

The Economic Times: https://economictimes.indiatimes.com/

The Hindu Business Line: https://www.thehindubusinessline.com/

McKinsey & Company: https://www.mckinsey.com/

World Economic Forum: https://www.weforum.org/

United Nations Development Programme (UNDP): https://www.undp.org/

3

SECURITY

In today's interconnected world, national security is a pressing concern for every nation, including Bharat. As a teenager, I recognize the importance of safeguarding Bharat's sovereignty, territorial integrity, and citizens' well-being in an increasingly complex geopolitical landscape. This essay explores matters of national security from a teenager's perspective, focusing on how Bharat can ensure its safety through diplomacy and defense strategies.

1. Understanding National Security:

National security encompasses a wide range of threats, including military aggression, terrorism, cyberattacks, natural disasters, and pandemics. Securing Bharat's borders, maintaining internal stability, and protecting critical infrastructure are vital aspects of national security.

2. Diplomacy:

a. Importance of Diplomacy: Diplomacy plays a crucial role in advancing Bharat's national security interests by building alliances, resolving conflicts, and promoting peace and cooperation. Diplomatic initiatives strengthen Bharat's relationships with neighboring countries and major global powers, contributing to regional stability and security.

b. Track Record of Diplomacy: Bharat has a long history of diplomatic engagement, characterized by its policy of non-alignment, active participation in international organizations, and commitment to multilateralism. Diplomatic efforts such as the Non-Aligned Movement (NAM), SAARC, and BRICS have bolstered Bharat's influence and promoted regional cooperation.

c. Challenges and Opportunities: Bharat faces various diplomatic challenges, including territorial disputes, cross-border terrorism, and geopolitical rivalries. However, diplomacy also offers opportunities for Bharat to address these challenges through dialogue, negotiation, and conflict resolution mechanisms.

3. Defense:

a. **Military Strength:** Bharat maintains a formidable defense force comprising the Indian Army, Navy, Air Force, and paramilitary units. With over 1.4 million active personnel, Bharat ranks among the largest military powers globally.

b. **Modernization Efforts:** Bharat is actively modernizing its defense capabilities through indigenous research and development, defense acquisitions, and technology partnerships. Initiatives such as Make in Bharat and Atmanirbhar Bharat aim to enhance self-reliance in defense production and reduce dependence on imports.

c. **Border Security:** Securing Bharat's borders is a top priority for national security. Bharat faces security challenges along its borders with Pakistan, China, and other neighboring countries, necessitating robust border management strategies and surveillance measures.

d. **Counterterrorism:** Bharat remains vigilant against the threat of terrorism, both domestically and internationally. The Mumbai attacks in 2008 and the Pulwama attack in 2019 underscore the importance of counterterrorism efforts in safeguarding Bharat's security and stability.

4. Role of Youth in National Security:

As teenagers, we have a stake in Bharat's national security and a responsibility to contribute to its protection. While we may not be directly involved in defense operations, we can play a role in promoting peace, tolerance, and unity within our communities. Additionally, we can advocate for policies that prioritize national security, support our armed forces, and foster a culture of resilience and preparedness.

5. Conclusion:

In conclusion, national security is a collective responsibility that requires a multifaceted approach encompassing diplomacy, defense, and societal resilience. As teenagers, we recognize the importance of diplomacy in advancing Bharat's interests and the need for a strong defense to protect against external threats. By actively engaging in discussions on national security issues, advocating for peace and stability, and supporting our armed forces, we can contribute to Bharat's safety and prosperity in an increasingly complex world.

- **_Sources:_**
1. _Ministry of External Affairs, Government of India: https://www.mea.gov.in/_
2. _Ministry of Defence, Government of India: https://mod.gov.in/_
3. _Institute for Defence Studies and Analyses (IDSA): https://idsa.in/_
4. _Observer Research Foundation (ORF): https://www.orfonline.org/_
5. _The Hindu: https://www.thehindu.com/_
6. _India Today: https://www.indiatoday.in/_
7. _Stockholm International Peace Research Institute (SIPRI): https://www.sipri.org/_
8. _Global Terrorism Database: https://www.start.umd.edu/gtd/_
9. _RAND Corporation: https://www.rand.org/_
10. _Pew Research Center: https://www.pewresearch.org/_

4

SCIENCE

&

TECHNOLOGY

1. Introduction to Innovation in Bharat:

Bharat has the potential to become a global leader in innovation by leveraging its rich scientific and technological capabilities, fostering a culture of entrepreneurship, and investing in research and development (R&D) across various sectors. Innovation is crucial for driving economic growth, enhancing competitiveness, and addressing pressing societal challenges.

2. Strategies for Becoming a Leader in Innovation:

a. Investment in Research and Development: Bharat must prioritize investment in R&D to foster innovation across sectors such as healthcare, agriculture, renewable energy, and information technology. Increasing public and private sector spending on R&D infrastructure, talent development, and collaborative research initiatives is essential to stimulate innovation.

b. Promotion of Entrepreneurship:

Encouraging entrepreneurship and startups is vital for fostering innovation ecosystems in Bharat. Creating conducive regulatory frameworks, providing access to finance and mentorship, and promoting industry-academia collaboration can support aspiring entrepreneurs and facilitate the commercialization of innovative ideas.

c. Enhancing Collaboration:

Collaboration between government, academia, industry, and research institutions is critical for driving innovation in Bharat. Establishing innovation clusters, technology parks, and incubators can facilitate knowledge exchange, networking, and collaboration among stakeholders.

d. *Skills Development:* Developing a skilled workforce equipped with the latest knowledge and technologies is essential for driving innovation in Bharat. Strengthening STEM (science, technology, engineering, and mathematics) education, vocational training, and lifelong learning programs can nurture talent and promote innovation-driven growth.

3. *Scientific Advancements Crucial for Bharat's Future:*

a. *Space Technology:* Bharat's space program, led by the Indian Space Research Organisation (ISRO), has achieved significant milestones in space exploration, satellite communication, and remote sensing. ISRO's successful missions to Mars (Mangalyaan) and the Moon (Chandrayaan) demonstrate Bharat's prowess in space technology.

Source:

Indian Space Research Organisation (ISRO): https://www.isro.gov.in/

b. *Technological Developments in Agriculture:*

In agriculture, technological advancements such as precision farming, drone technology, biotechnology, and digital agriculture hold immense potential for enhancing productivity, reducing wastage, and ensuring food security in Bharat.

Source:

Ministry of Agriculture and Farmers Welfare, Government of India: https://agricoop.nic.in/

c. Alternative Energy Sources:

Bharat is investing in renewable energy sources such as solar, wind, and bioenergy to reduce dependence on fossil fuels, mitigate climate change, and promote sustainable development. The National Solar Mission aims to achieve 100 GW of solar power capacity by 2022.

Sources:

Ministry of New and Renewable Energy, Government of India: https://mnre.gov.in/

International Solar Alliance: https://isolaralliance.org/

4. Impact of Scientific Advancements on Bharat's Economy and Society:

a. Space Technology:

Bharat's space program has contributed to technological innovation, national security, disaster management, and socio-economic development. Satellite-based services in telecommunication, navigation, weather forecasting, and agriculture benefit various sectors of the economy.

b. Technological Developments in Agriculture:

Innovations in agriculture technology have the potential to revolutionize farming practices, increase agricultural productivity, improve farmer livelihoods, and ensure food security for Bharat's growing population.

c. Alternative Energy Sources:

The adoption of renewable energy sources contributes to energy security, reduces greenhouse gas emissions, creates employment opportunities, and promotes sustainable development in Bharat.

5. Conclusion:

In conclusion, Bharat has the potential to become a global leader in innovation by investing in research and development, promoting entrepreneurship, enhancing collaboration, and developing a skilled workforce. Scientific advancements in space technology, agriculture, and alternative energy sources are crucial for driving economic growth, addressing societal challenges, and ensuring sustainable development in Bharat. By harnessing its scientific and technological capabilities, Bharat can emerge as a trailblazer in innovation and contribute to shaping a brighter future for its citizens and the world.

Sources:

1. *Indian Space Research Organisation (ISRO): https://www.isro.gov.in/*

2. *Ministry of Agriculture and Farmers Welfare, Government of India: https://agricoop.nic.in/*

3. *Ministry of New and Renewable Energy, Government of India: https://mnre.gov.in/*

4. *International Solar Alliance: https://isolaralliance.org/*

5. *The Economic Times: https://economictimes.indiatimes.com/*

6. *NITI Aayog: https://niti.gov.in/*

7. *World Bank: https://www.worldbank.org/en/country/india/overview*

8. *Reserve Bank of India: https://www.rbi.org.in/*

9. *McKinsey & Company: https://www.mckinsey.com/*

10. *United Nations Development Programme (UNDP): https://www.undp.org/*

5
SOCIETY
&
CULTURE

To thoroughly explore how Bharat's rich cultural heritage can be leveraged on the world stage and its impact on various societal issues such as education, healthcare, and women's empowerment, we need to delve into several aspects of its society and culture. This comprehensive analysis will include discussions on the importance of preserving cultural heritage, promoting inclusive education and healthcare systems, and advancing gender equality. Additionally, we will incorporate relevant data and sources to support our arguments and provide a well-rounded perspective on shaping a new Bharat.

1. Introduction: Leveraging Bharat's Cultural Heritage on the World Stage

Bharat's cultural heritage is rich and diverse, encompassing a tapestry of traditions, languages, arts, and spiritual practices that span thousands of years. This cultural wealth not only defines Bharat's identity but also serves as a source of pride and soft power on the global stage. Leveraging Bharat's cultural heritage effectively can enhance its international standing, foster cross-cultural understanding, and promote economic development through tourism, cultural exchanges, and creative industries.

2. Preserving Cultural Heritage:

a. Cultural Tourism: Bharat's cultural heritage sites, such as the Taj Mahal, Qutub Minar, and Ajanta-Ellora caves, attract millions of tourists from around the world each year. Promoting sustainable tourism and preserving these iconic landmarks can generate revenue, create jobs, and boost local economies while safeguarding cultural heritage for future generations.

b. **Traditional Arts and Crafts:** Bharat's traditional arts and crafts, including pottery, weaving, painting, and sculpture, are part of its cultural legacy. Supporting artisans, craftsmen, and traditional art forms through skill development, marketing initiatives, and cultural festivals can revitalize these industries and promote cultural diversity.

c. **Language and Literature:** Bharat is home to a myriad of languages and literary traditions, from Sanskrit epics like the Ramayana and Mahabharata to regional languages like Tamil, Bengali, and Marathi. Promoting language preservation, literary festivals, and translations can enrich global literature and foster cross-cultural dialogue.

3. Inclusive Education:

a. Quality Education for All:

Bharat's education system plays a crucial role in shaping its future. However, disparities in access to quality education persist, particularly in rural and marginalized communities. Investing in infrastructure, teacher training, and curriculum reform can improve educational outcomes and empower youth to realize their full potential.

b. Cultural Education:

Integrating cultural education into the curriculum can foster a sense of pride and belonging among students while promoting intercultural understanding and tolerance. Teaching Bharat's diverse cultural heritage can instill values of empathy, respect, and inclusivity from a young age.

c. Digital Learning:

Embracing digital technologies and e-learning platforms can expand access to education, particularly in remote areas where physical infrastructure is lacking. Initiatives such as Digital Bharat and online educational resources can bridge the digital divide and democratize access to knowledge.

4. Healthcare Access and Equity:

a. Universal Healthcare:

Bharat's healthcare system faces challenges in terms of access, affordability, and quality of care. Implementing universal healthcare coverage, strengthening primary healthcare services, and investing in preventive health measures can improve health outcomes and reduce disparities.

b. Traditional Medicine:

Bharat has a rich tradition of traditional medicine systems such as Ayurveda, Yoga, and Naturopathy. Integrating traditional medicine into mainstream healthcare practices can enhance holistic health and wellness, complementing modern medical interventions.

c. Women's Health:

Addressing women's health issues, including maternal mortality, reproductive health, and gender-based violence, is essential for achieving gender equality and social development. Investing in women's healthcare services, promoting reproductive rights, and empowering women as health advocates can improve overall societal well-being.

5. Women's Empowerment:

a. Education and Employment: Empowering women through education, skill development, and economic opportunities is key to unlocking their full potential. Providing access to quality education, vocational training, and entrepreneurship programs can enhance women's economic independence and decision-making power.

b. Political Representation: Increasing women's political participation and representation in decision-making bodies can ensure that their voices are heard and their rights are protected. Implementing gender quotas, promoting women's leadership training, and supporting women in politics can advance gender equality in governance.

c. Legal Reforms: Enacting and enforcing laws to combat gender-based discrimination, violence, and inequality is essential for creating a more equitable society. Strengthening legal frameworks, providing access to justice, and raising awareness about women's rights can drive societal change and foster gender-sensitive attitudes.

6. Conclusion: Shaping a New Bharat

In conclusion, leveraging Bharat's rich cultural heritage on the world stage and addressing societal issues such as education, healthcare, and women's empowerment are integral to shaping a new Bharat that is inclusive, prosperous, and globally respected. By preserving cultural heritage, promoting inclusive education and healthcare systems, and advancing gender equality, Bharat can harness its full potential and emerge as a leader in the 21st century. It is imperative for policymakers, civil society organizations, and individuals to work together to build a more equitable and sustainable future for Bharat and its citizens.

Sources:

1. Ministry of Culture, Government of Bharat: https://www.indiaculture.nic.in/
2. Ministry of Education, Government of Bharat: https://www.education.gov.in/
3. Ministry of Health and Family Welfare, Government of Bharat: https://www.mohfw.gov.in/
4. United Nations Educational, Scientific and Cultural Organization (UNESCO): https://en.unesco.org/
5. World Health Organization (WHO): https://www.who.int/
6. National Institution for Transforming Bharat (NITI Aayog): https://niti.gov.in/
7. United Nations Development Programme (UNDP): https://www.undp.org/
8. Bharat Brand Equity Foundation (IBEF): https://www.ibef.org/
9. Census of Bharat: https://censusindia.gov.in/
10. Global Gender Gap Report, World Economic Forum: https://www.weforum.org/reports/global-gender-gap-report-2020

6

ENVIRONMENT

Bharat faces significant environmental challenges that threaten the health and well-being of its citizens, ecosystems, and future generations. These challenges include air and water pollution, deforestation, habitat loss, climate change, and resource depletion. However, Bharat also has the potential to become a leader in sustainability by implementing innovative solutions, embracing renewable energy sources, and adopting effective pollution control measures. This article explores Bharat's environmental challenges, outlines strategies for leadership in sustainability, and examines the role of renewable energy and pollution control measures in mitigating environmental degradation.

1. Environmental Challenges in Bharat:

a. Air Pollution:

Bharat's air quality is among the poorest in the world, with major cities facing severe pollution levels. Sources of air pollution include vehicular emissions, industrial activities, construction dust, biomass burning, and agricultural practices. Poor air quality contributes to respiratory diseases, cardiovascular problems, and premature deaths.

b. Water Pollution:

Bharat's water bodies are contaminated with pollutants such as untreated sewage, industrial effluents, agricultural runoff, and chemical waste. Water pollution threatens public health, biodiversity, and aquatic ecosystems, leading to waterborne diseases, habitat degradation, and loss of aquatic species.

c. Deforestation and Habitat Loss:

Bharat has witnessed significant deforestation and habitat loss due to urbanization, agricultural expansion, logging, and infrastructure development. Deforestation leads to loss of biodiversity, soil erosion, flooding, and climate change impacts such as reduced carbon sequestration and altered rainfall patterns.

d. Climate Change:

Bharat is vulnerable to the impacts of climate change, including extreme weather events, rising temperatures, changing precipitation patterns, and sea-level rise. Climate change exacerbates existing environmental challenges and poses risks to agriculture, water resources, coastal communities, and vulnerable populations.

e. Resource Depletion:

Bharat's rapid economic growth and industrialization have resulted in the depletion of natural resources such as land, water, minerals, and forests. Unsustainable resource extraction practices threaten ecosystem integrity, biodiversity, and long-term sustainability.

2. Strategies for Leadership in Sustainability:

a. Renewable Energy Transition:

Bharat has the potential to become a global leader in renewable energy by harnessing its abundant solar, wind, hydro, and biomass resources. Investing in renewable energy infrastructure, promoting clean energy technologies, and incentivizing renewable energy adoption can accelerate the transition towards a low-carbon economy.

b. Green Infrastructure Development:

Bharat can promote sustainable urbanization and green infrastructure development to address air and water pollution, mitigate climate change impacts, and enhance resilience to environmental hazards. Green infrastructure solutions include green buildings, sustainable transportation, urban parks, and rooftop gardens.

c. Sustainable Agriculture Practices:

Bharat can promote sustainable agriculture practices such as organic farming, agroforestry, crop diversification, and water-efficient irrigation techniques. Sustainable agriculture enhances soil health, biodiversity, and ecosystem services while reducing greenhouse gas emissions and chemical pollution.

d. Biodiversity Conservation:

Protecting biodiversity hotspots, wildlife habitats, and natural ecosystems is essential for biodiversity conservation and ecosystem restoration. Bharat can establish protected areas, wildlife corridors, and community-based conservation initiatives to safeguard biodiversity and restore degraded ecosystems.

4. Role of Renewable Energy Sources:

a. Solar Energy:

Bharat has abundant solar energy potential, with over 300 days of sunshine annually. The Bharatn government's ambitious solar energy targets aim to install 100 GW of solar capacity by 2022 and 450 GW by 2030. Solar energy can provide clean and sustainable electricity while reducing greenhouse gas emissions and dependence on fossil fuels.

b. Wind Energy:

Bharat ranks among the top wind energy producers globally, with significant wind power potential along its coastline and in inland regions. The Bharatn government aims to achieve 60 GW of wind energy capacity by 2022. Wind energy is a cost-effective and environmentally friendly renewable energy source that can contribute to Bharat's energy security and climate goals.

c. Hydropower:

Bharat has significant hydropower potential, primarily in the Himalayan region and northeastern states. Hydropower projects can provide clean and renewable electricity while supporting water management, irrigation, and flood control. However, hydropower development must be balanced with environmental and social considerations to minimize negative impacts on ecosystems and local communities.

d. Biomass Energy:

Biomass energy from agricultural residues, forest biomass, and organic waste can provide decentralized and renewable energy solutions for rural areas. Biomass energy technologies such as biogas plants, biomass gasification, and biomass-based power generation can promote rural development, energy access, and sustainable waste management.

5. Pollution Control Measures:

a. Air Pollution Control:

Bharat has implemented various measures to control air pollution, including the Indian National Clean Air Programme (NCAP), vehicle emission standards, industrial pollution control regulations, and promotion of clean technologies. Strengthening enforcement mechanisms, investing in public transportation, and promoting clean energy alternatives can further improve air quality.

b. Water Pollution Control:

Bharat is taking steps to address water pollution through measures such as the Clean Ganga Mission, wastewater treatment plants, river conservation programs, and water quality monitoring initiatives. Integrated water resource management, pollution prevention measures, and community participation are essential for sustainable water management and pollution control.

c. Waste Management:

Bharat is implementing waste management initiatives to reduce waste generation, promote recycling and composting, and improve solid waste management practices. The Swachh Bharat Mission aims to achieve universal sanitation and cleanliness by 2022, contributing to improved public health and environmental sustainability.

6. Conclusion:

In conclusion, Bharat faces significant environmental challenges, including air and water pollution, deforestation, climate change, and resource depletion. However, Bharat also has the potential to become a leader in sustainability by implementing innovative solutions, embracing renewable energy sources, and adopting effective pollution control measures. By prioritizing environmental conservation, promoting sustainable development, and fostering international cooperation, Bharat can achieve its environmental goals and contribute to a more sustainable and resilient future for the planet.

Sources:

1. Ministry of Environment, Forest and Climate Change, Bharat: http://moef.gov.in/
2. Central Pollution Control Board, India: https://cpcb.nic.in/
3. Indian Renewable Energy Development Agency (IREDA): https://ireda.gov.in/
4. International Energy Agency (IEA): https://www.iea.org/
5. United Nations Environment Programme (UNEP): https://www.unep.org/
6. World Bank: https://www.worldbank.org/en/country/india/overview
7. Indian Institute of Science (IISc): https://www.iisc.ac.in/
8. IndianSpace Research Organisation (ISRO): https://www.isro.gov.in/
9. Ministry of New and Renewable Energy, Bharat: https://mnre.gov.in/
10. IndianCouncil of Agricultural Research (ICAR): https://www.icar.org.in/

7

VISION FOR

THE FUTURE

Bharat's geopolitical future is shaped by a complex interplay of domestic factors, regional dynamics, and global trends. As one of the world's largest and fastest-growing economies, Bharat holds immense potential to emerge as a key player on the global stage. However, it also faces numerous challenges that must be addressed to realize this potential fully.

Key Points about Bharat's Geopolitical Future:

1. Economic Growth:

Bharat's economic growth trajectory is crucial for its geopolitical positioning. With a GDP expected to surpass major economies in the coming decades, including Japan, Germany, and even the United States, Bharat is poised to become a formidable economic power. However, sustaining this growth requires addressing structural challenges such as income inequality, infrastructure deficits, and bureaucratic hurdles.

2. Regional Dynamics:

Bharat's relationships with neighboring countries and regional powers play a significant role in shaping its geopolitical future. Tensions with Pakistan and China, as well as strategic partnerships with countries like the United States and Japan, impact Bharat's security and influence in South Asia and beyond.

3. Global Influence:

Bharat's rising global influence is evident in its participation in international forums such as the G20, BRICS, and the United Nations. As the world's largest democracy and a vocal advocate for multilateralism, Bharat has the potential to shape global governance and address pressing global challenges, including climate change, terrorism, and pandemics.

4. Strategic Partnerships:

Strengthening strategic partnerships with key countries and regional blocs is crucial for Bharat's geopolitical positioning. Enhancing defense cooperation, economic ties, and diplomatic engagement with allies and partners can bolster Bharat's security and promote its interests in the Indo-Pacific region and beyond.

5. Technology and Innovation:

Embracing technology and innovation is essential for Bharat to maintain its competitive edge in the global economy. Investing in research and development, fostering a culture of entrepreneurship, and leveraging digital technologies can drive economic growth, enhance productivity, and promote Bharat's leadership in emerging industries.

Reiteration of Hope and Vision for Bharat as a Teen:

As a teenager, I am optimistic about Bharat's future and envision a Bharat that is prosperous, inclusive, and globally influential. My hope is for Bharat to harness its immense potential to uplift its citizens, promote peace and stability, and contribute to global progress.

Call to Action - Inspire Others to Get Involved in Shaping Bharat's Future:

I urge my fellow teenagers and citizens of Bharat to actively engage in shaping the country's future. Whether through education, innovation, civic participation, or advocacy, each one of us has a role to play in building a better Bharat. Let us come together, transcend barriers, and work towards a shared vision of a Bharat that is prosperous, peaceful, and progressive. Together, we can shape Bharat's geopolitical future and leave a positive legacy for generations to come.

<u>**Sources**</u>:

1. World Bank: https://www.worldbank.org/en/country/india/overview
2. Reserve Bank of India: https://www.rbi.org.in/
3. Ministry of Commerce and Industry, Government of India: https://commerce.gov.in/
4. NITI Aayog: https://niti.gov.in/
5. International Monetary Fund (IMF): https://www.imf.org/en/Countries/IND
6. The Economic Times: https://economictimes.indiatimes.com/
7. The Hindu Business Line: https://www.thehindubusinessline.com/
8. McKinsey & Company: https://www.mckinsey.com/
9. World Economic Forum: https://www.weforum.org/
10. United Nations Development Programme (UNDP): https://www.undp.org/

8

CONCLUSION

Summary of Bharat's Geopolitical Future:

Bharat's geopolitical future is influenced by various factors, including its economic growth, strategic location, military capabilities, diplomatic relations, and cultural influence. As a rising power, Bharat aims to assert its influence regionally and globally while navigating complex geopolitical dynamics. The country's geopolitical future will be shaped by its ability to balance competing interests, strengthen alliances, address security challenges, promote economic cooperation, and uphold its values on the world stage.

Key Points:

1. Economic Growth:

Bharat's rapid economic growth and demographic dividend position it as a significant player in the global economy. With a GDP expected to reach $5 trillion by 2024, Bharat aims to leverage its economic strength to enhance its geopolitical influence (Source: Ministry of Finance, Government of India).

2. Strategic Location:

Bharat's strategic location in South Asia makes it a key player in regional geopolitics. As a maritime nation, Bharat's proximity to vital sea lanes of communication gives it strategic importance in global trade and security (Source: Indian Navy).

3. Military Capabilities:

Bharat's military capabilities, including its army, navy, and air force, play a crucial role in shaping its geopolitical future. With modernization efforts and defense partnerships, Bharat aims to enhance its security posture and contribute to regional stability (Source: Ministry of Defence, Government of India).

4. Diplomatic Relations:

Bharat's diplomatic engagements with neighboring countries, major powers, and international organizations are instrumental in shaping its geopolitical strategy. Diplomatic initiatives such as Act East Policy, Neighborhood First Policy, and Indo-Pacific Strategy aim to foster regional cooperation and enhance Bharat's influence (Source: Ministry of External Affairs, Government of India).

5. Cultural Influence:

Bharat's rich cultural heritage, soft power assets, and diaspora contribute to its influence on the global stage. Cultural diplomacy, promotion of yoga, Ayurveda, and Bollywood, and the Indian diaspora's role as cultural ambassadors enhance Bharat's global presence and influence (Source: Ministry of Culture, Government of India).

Hope and Vision for Bharat as a Teen:

As a teenager, my hope and vision for Bharat are rooted in the belief that it can emerge as a beacon of democracy, diversity, and development on the world stage. I envision Bharat as a nation that upholds the principles of inclusivity, sustainability, and social justice while playing a constructive role in addressing global challenges.

My hope for Bharat is that it will continue to harness its economic potential, invest in human capital, and foster innovation and entrepreneurship to drive sustainable growth and development. I envision Bharat as a leader in technology, science, and innovation, contributing to global knowledge creation and solving pressing societal challenges.

Furthermore, I believe in Bharat's ability to promote peace, cooperation, and dialogue in its neighborhood and beyond. By fostering strong diplomatic relations, promoting regional integration, and championing multilateralism, Bharat can contribute to a more stable and prosperous world.

Call to Action:

I urge my fellow citizens, especially the youth, to actively engage in shaping Bharat's future. We must seize the opportunities presented by globalization, technology, and international cooperation to build a stronger, more resilient Bharat.

Here are some ways we can get involved:

1. Education and Skill Development:

Invest in education, acquire relevant skills, and pursue lifelong learning to contribute to Bharat's knowledge economy.

2. Innovation and Entrepreneurship:

Foster innovation, start new ventures, and create solutions to societal challenges to drive economic growth and job creation.

3. Civic Engagement:

Participate in democratic processes, advocate for policy reforms, and engage in community service to contribute to Bharat's development.

4. Diplomacy and International Relations:

Promote people-to-people diplomacy, cultural exchange, and constructive dialogue to enhance Bharat's global reputation and influence.

5. Environmental Stewardship:

Adopt sustainable practices, support environmental conservation efforts, and advocate for policies that address climate change and protect natural resources.

By coming together as a nation and harnessing our collective talents, energy, and aspirations, we can shape a brighter future for Bharat and contribute to a more peaceful, prosperous, and inclusive world.

Sources:

1. Ministry of Finance, Government of India - https://www.indiabudget.gov.in/
2. Indian Navy - https://www.indiannavy.nic.in/
3. Ministry of Defence, Government of India - https://mod.gov.in/
4. Ministry of External Affairs, Government of India - https://mea.gov.in/
5. Ministry of Culture, Government of India - https://www.indiaculture.nic.in

9

PERSPECTIVE OF A TEEN

Introduction to Bharat's Economic Landscape.

As a teenager growing up in Bharat, I am keenly aware of the economic opportunities and challenges that shape our nation's future. Bharat, with its vast population and diverse economy, holds immense potential for growth and development. However, it also faces numerous obstacles that hinder its progress. In this chapter, we will explore Bharat's economic strengths and weaknesses, as well as strategies for unlocking its full potential.

Bharat's Economic Strengths:

1. Market Size:

Bharat's large population of over 1.3 billion people makes it one of the largest consumer markets in the world. This vast market size presents significant opportunities for businesses across various sectors, driving demand and economic growth.

According to data from the World Bank, Bharat's GDP stood at $2.87 trillion in 2020, making it the fifth-largest economy globally. With a growing middle class and increasing urbanization, consumer spending is expected to continue rising, fueling economic expansion.

2. Young Workforce:

Bharat has a demographic dividend, with a youthful population that provides a significant advantage in terms of labor force participation and productivity. According to the United Nations, Bharat's median age is around 28 years, compared to 38 years for China and 38.1 years for the United States.

This youthful workforce presents opportunities for innovation, entrepreneurship, and economic dynamism. However, harnessing this demographic dividend requires investments in education, skill development, and job creation.

3. Diverse Economy:

Bharat's economy is diverse, with strengths in agriculture, manufacturing, services, and information technology. This diversification helps mitigate risks and ensures resilience against external shocks. According to the Reserve Bank of Bharat, the services sector accounts for around 55% of GDP, followed by industry (30%) and agriculture (15%).

The services sector, particularly information technology and business process outsourcing, has emerged as a key driver of economic growth and employment generation. However, Bharat also faces challenges such as income inequality, infrastructure deficits, bureaucratic hurdles, and a high rate of informal employment.

Bharat's Economic Weaknesses:

1. Income Inequality:

Despite economic growth, Bharat grapples with significant income inequality, with a large portion of the population still living below the poverty line. According to data from the World Inequality Database, the richest 10% of Bharat's population holds over 77% of the country's total wealth, while the bottom 50% holds just 4.1%.

This inequality poses social challenges and hampers inclusive growth. Addressing income inequality requires targeted policies aimed at reducing poverty, improving access to education and healthcare, and promoting inclusive economic development.

2. Infrastructure Deficits:

Bharat faces infrastructure deficits in areas such as transportation, energy, and urban development. According to the World Economic Forum's Global Competitiveness Report, Bharat ranks 70th out of 141 countries in terms of infrastructure quality.

Inadequate infrastructure hinders productivity, increases logistics costs, and limits the potential for economic expansion. Addressing infrastructure deficits requires investments in roads, railways, ports, airports, energy, and digital connectivity.

3. Bureaucratic Hurdles:

Complex regulatory frameworks, bureaucratic red tape, and a slow decision-making process impede business growth and investment in Bharat. According to the World Bank's Ease of Doing Business Index, Bharat ranks 63rd out of 190 countries in terms of ease of doing business.

Streamlining administrative processes, reducing regulatory burden, and improving governance are essential to foster a more business-friendly environment. The Bharatn government has launched initiatives such as Digital Bharat and Make in Bharat to promote ease of doing business and attract investment.

4. Informal Employment:

A significant portion of Bharat's workforce is employed in the informal sector, lacking job security, social protection, and access to formal financial services. According to the International Labour Organization (ILO), around 81% of Bharat's employed population is engaged in informal employment.

Formalizing the informal economy is crucial to improve labor productivity, promote decent work, and ensure social protection for workers. This requires measures such as skill development, social security schemes, and financial inclusion initiatives.

Strategies for Strengthening Bharat's Economy:

1. Investment in Infrastructure:

Bharat must prioritize investment in infrastructure development to address deficits and unlock growth potential. This includes enhancing transportation networks, expanding energy infrastructure, and improving urban amenities.

According to the Asian Development Bank (ADB), Bharat requires an estimated $4.5 trillion in infrastructure investment by 2040 to sustain its economic growth trajectory. Public-private partnerships (PPPs), foreign direct investment (FDI), and multilateral financing can help bridge the infrastructure financing gap.

2. Skill Development and Education:

Investing in education and skill development is essential to harness Bharat's demographic dividend. Enhancing access to quality education, vocational training, and lifelong learning opportunities can equip the workforce with the skills needed for the future economy.

According to the National Skill Development Corporation (NSDC), Bharat faces a shortage of skilled workers across various sectors, including manufacturing, healthcare, and information technology. Skill development initiatives such as Pradhan Mantri Kaushal Vikas Yojana (PMKVY) aim to bridge this gap and enhance employability.

3. Ease of Doing Business Reforms:

Bharat should focus on simplifying regulatory processes, reducing bureaucratic hurdles, and improving the ease of doing business. Creating a conducive environment for entrepreneurship and investment will spur innovation, job creation, and economic growth.

The Bharatn government has undertaken several reforms to improve the ease of doing business, including the introduction of online single-window clearances, faster approvals for licenses and permits, and digitization of administrative processes. These efforts have led to Bharat's significant improvement in the World Bank's Ease of Doing Business rankings in recent years.

4. Promotion of Digital Economy:

Embracing digital technologies and promoting digital literacy can unlock new opportunities for Bharat's economy. Digital initiatives such as Digital Bharat, Make in Bharat, and Bharat Stack aim to digitize processes, improve efficiency, and foster innovation across sectors.

According to a report by McKinsey & Company, digital technologies have the potential to create up to $1 trillion of economic value in Bharat by 2025. Promoting digital payments, e-commerce, and digital infrastructure can drive inclusive growth, empower small businesses, and create new employment opportunities.

Impact of Globalization and Trade on Bharat's Economy:

1. Trade Liberalization:
Bharat has witnessed significant trade liberalization reforms over the past few decades, leading to increased integration into the global economy. Trade agreements such as the Comprehensive Economic Partnership Agreement (CEPA) and Regional Comprehensive Economic Partnership (RCEP) aim to enhance trade relations and boost exports.

According to data from the Ministry of Commerce and Industry, Bharat's merchandise exports stood at $290.63 billion in 2020-21, with top export destinations including the United States, China, and the United Arab Emirates. However, Bharat also faces challenges such as trade deficits, currency fluctuations, and non-tariff barriers in global markets.

2. Foreign Direct Investment (FDI):
Globalization has facilitated greater inflows of foreign direct investment (FDI)

into Bharat, particularly in sectors such as information technology, manufacturing, and services. FDI inflows contribute to capital formation, technology transfer, and job creation in Bharat.

According to data from the Reserve Bank of Bharat, FDI inflows into Bharat stood at $81.72 billion in 2020-21, despite the economic challenges posed by the COVID-19 pandemic. The services sector attracted the highest share of FDI inflows, followed by computer software and hardware, telecommunications, and trading.

3. Global Value Chains:

Bharat is increasingly participating in global value chains (GVCs), whereby goods and services are produced across different countries, creating efficiencies and specialization. Integration into GVCs offers opportunities for Bharat to enhance competitiveness, access new markets, and upgrade technology.

According to a report by the World Trade Organization (WTO), Bharat's participation in GVCs has increased significantly in recent years, driven by sectors such as automotive, electronics, and textiles. However, Bharat also faces challenges such as supply chain disruptions, regulatory barriers, and skills shortages in fully leveraging the potential of GVCs.

4. Challenges of Protectionism:

However, Bharat also faces challenges posed by rising protectionism and trade tensions in the global arena. Trade disputes, tariffs, and non-tariff barriers hinder Bharat's export-oriented growth and disrupt supply chains.

According to a report by the United Nations Conference on Trade and Development (UNCTAD), global trade tensions, particularly between major economies such as the United States and China, have intensified in recent years. Bharat must navigate these challenges through diplomacy, diversification of export markets, and strengthening of domestic industries.

Conclusion: In conclusion, Bharat's economic landscape is characterized by significant strengths, including its large market size, young workforce, diverse economy, and entrepreneurial culture. However, it also faces challenges such as income inequality, infrastructure deficits, bureaucratic hurdles, and informal employment. To become a stronger economic power, Bharat must prioritize investments in infrastructure, education, and skill development, streamline regulatory processes, and promote innovation and entrepreneurship.

Globalization and trade present both opportunities and challenges for Bharat's economy. While trade liberalization, FDI inflows, and participation in global value chains offer opportunities for growth and integration, rising protectionism and trade tensions pose risks to Bharat's export-oriented growth model. Addressing these challenges requires proactive policies, strategic reforms, and international cooperation to navigate the complexities of the global economy and ensure sustainable economic development for Bharat.

<u>Sources:</u>

1. *World Bank: https://www.worldbank.org/en/country/india/overview*
2. *Reserve Bank of Bharat: https://www.rbi.org.in/*
3. *Ministry of Commerce and Industry, Government of Bharat: https://commerce.gov.in/*
4. *NITI Aayog: https://niti.gov.in/*
5. *International Monetary Fund (IMF): https://www.imf.org/en/Countries/IND*
6. *The Economic Times: https://economictimes.indiatimes.com/*
7. *The Hindu Business Line: https://www.thehindubusinessline.com/*
8. *McKinsey & Company: https://www.mckinsey.com/*
9. *World Economic Forum: https://www.weforum.org/*
10. *United Nations Development Programme (UNDP): https://www.undp.org/*
11. *United Nations Conference on Trade and Development (UNCTAD): https://unctad.org/*

BHARAT: REDEFINED GEOPOLITICALLY by PRANJAL GUHA